f

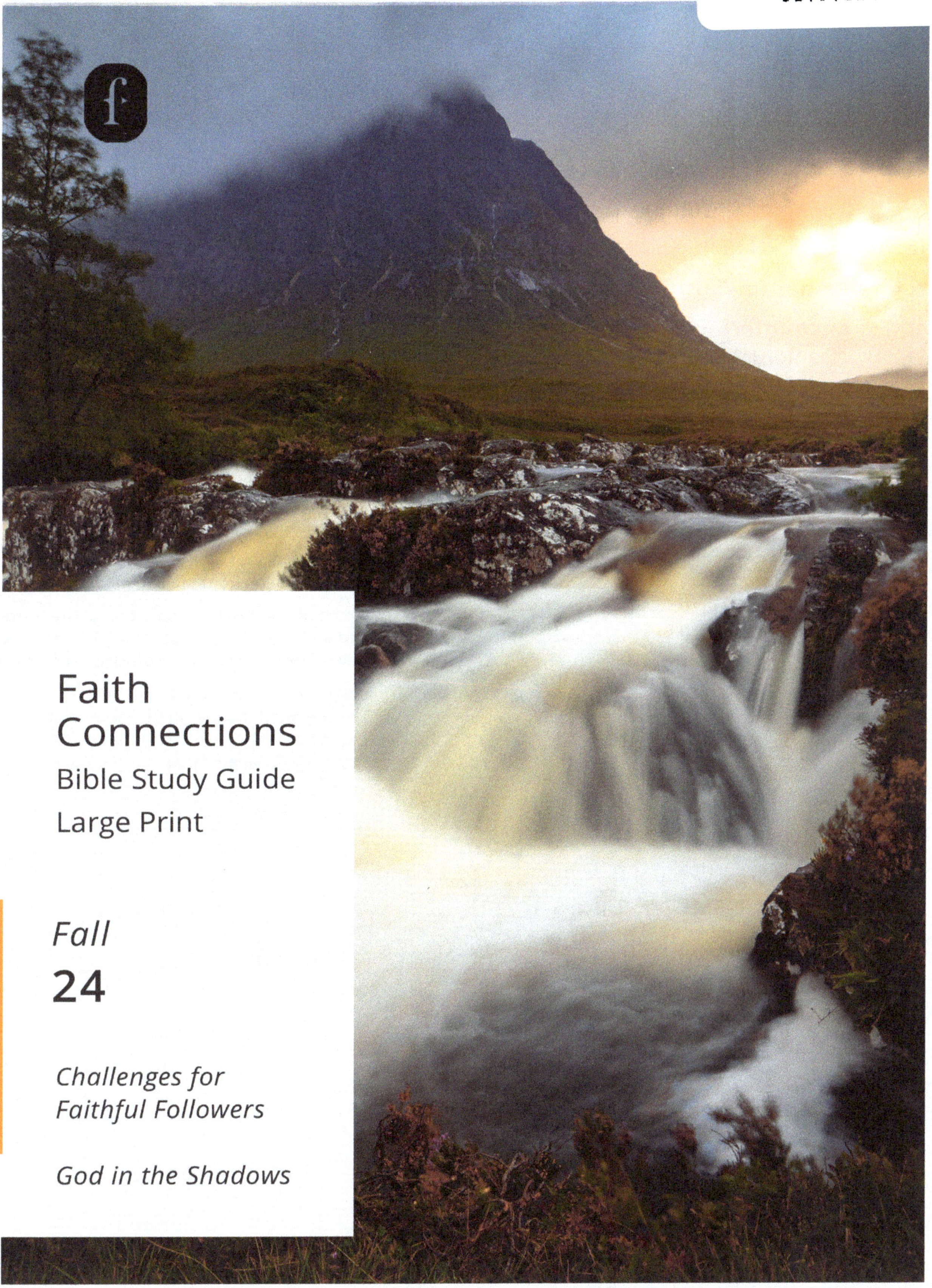

Faith Connections

Bible Study Guide

Large Print

Fall

24

Challenges for Faithful Followers

God in the Shadows

Bible Study Guide

Contents

Fall 2024
Volume 48, Number 1

Mike L. Wonch
Editor

Cover Photo: © Daniel_Kay/Shutterstock.com

All scripture quotations, unless otherwise indicated, are taken from the *Holy Bible, New International Version* (NIV). Copyright © 1973, 1978, 1984, 2011 by Biblica Inc. Used by permission. All rights reserved.

From the *New Revised Standard Version* (NRSV) of the Bible, copyright 1989 by the Division of Christian Education of the National Council of the Churches of Christ in the USA. Used by permission. All rights reserved.

All Scripture quotations marked † are the author's own translation from the original languages.

We believe in the full inspiration of the Scripture and encourage the comparison and use of several translations as part of the discipline of Bible study.

Bible Study Guide is published quarterly by The Foundry Publishing®, P.O. Box 419527, Kansas City, MO 64141. Copyright © 2024 by The Foundry Publishing®. Canadian GST No. R129017471.

Adult Bible Study Guide is one of several Faith Connections companion products, a themed suite of resources designed to help adults discover what it means to be holy people in today's world. To order, call 1-800-877-0700.

Perspectives

Take Heart! God Is at Work

Here is a riddle: *When you fall down, it's because of me. I hold you down, but for your own good. What am I?* Answer: Gravity. Gravity is "the force by which a planet or other body draws objects toward its center. The force of gravity keeps all of the planets in orbit around the sun."[1] Gravity is the reason why, when you jump up in the air, you come down rather than floating off into the atmosphere. It is the reason why, when things are dropped from a tall building, they plummet to the ground. We can't see gravity, but we know it's there and always at work.

A year ago, my wife and I took a weekend trip. While on our brief getaway, we went to a musical drama based on the story of Queen Esther. The presentation included live animals, elaborate staging, colorful costumes, and talented vocal performances. As amazing as all that was, the story is even more amazing. All through the production, I couldn't help but think how God was at work throughout the story, even when the central characters like Esther and Mordechai couldn't plainly see all the ways in which God was moving.

Throughout the Bible, we encounter stories of God working behind the scenes (e.g., Joseph; Jonah). In the story of Esther, it is not hard to see God's hand moving on behalf of His people. Despite how things looked outwardly, God was at work. Even the fact that we see God moving, yet He is not specifically mentioned in the story of Esther, testifies to God's sovereignty and providence. At one point in the story, Esther's cousin Mordecai tells her, "If you remain silent at this time, relief and deliverance for the Jews will arise from another place, but you and your father's family will perish. And who knows but that you have come to your royal position for such a time as this?" (Esther 4:14). Mordecai's statement points to the fact that God is always working in and through people and situations to accomplish His will.

Take heart! Even when we can't see it, or even feel it, God is moving. Today, may we be reminded that we must "live by faith, not by sight" (2 Corinthians 5:7), resting in the truth that God is at work.

May God bless you as you study His Word this quarter!

MIKE WONCH
Editor

1.<https://spaceplace.nasa.gov/what-is-gravity/en/> Accessed January 18, 2024.

ENCOUNTERING A HOSTILE CULTURE

God enables His people to live faithfully in a world that opposes His kingdom and seeks to lure them into its values.

THE WORD

DANIEL 1:1-10

In the third year of the reign of Jehoiakim king of Judah, Nebuchadnezzar king of Babylon came to Jerusalem and besieged it. 2And
the Lord delivered Jehoiakim king of Judah into his hand, along with
some of the articles from the temple of God. These he carried off to
the temple of his god in Babylonia and put in the treasure house of his
god.

3Then the king ordered Ashpenaz, chief of his court officials,
to bring into the king's service some of the Israelites from the royal
family and the nobility—4young men without any physical defect,
handsome, showing aptitude for every kind of learning, well informed,
quick to understand, and qualified to serve in the king's palace. He
was to teach them the language and literature of the Babylonians.
5The king assigned them a daily amount of food and wine from the
king's table. They were to be trained for three years, and after that
they were to enter the king's service.

6Among those who were chosen were some from Judah: Daniel,
Hananiah, Mishael and Azariah. 7The chief official gave them new
names: to Daniel, the name Belteshazzar; to Hananiah, Shadrach; to
Mishael, Meshach; and to Azariah, Abednego.

8But Daniel resolved not to defile himself with the royal food
and wine, and he asked the chief official for permission not to defile
himself this way. 9Now God had caused the official to show favor and
compassion to Daniel, 10but the official told Daniel, "I am afraid of my
lord the king, who has assigned your food and drink. Why should he
see you looking worse than the other young men your age? The king
would then have my head because of you."

17-20 **[17]To these four young men God gave knowledge and under-**
KEY VERSE **standing of all kinds of literature and learning. And Daniel could**
understand visions and dreams of all kinds.
[18]At the end of the time set by the king to bring them into his
service, the chief official presented them to Nebuchadnezzar. [19]The
king talked with them, and he found none equal to Daniel, Hananiah,
Mishael and Azariah; so they entered the king's service. [20]In every
matter of wisdom and understanding about which the king questioned
them, he found them ten times better than all the magicians and
enchanters in his whole kingdom.

ENGAGE THE WORD

THE HOSTILE CULTURE

Daniel 1:1-7

Daniel found himself swept into a hostile world over which he had little control. The powerful Babylonian armies had seized control of the ancient Middle East, including his hometown of Jerusalem in Judah. They took the best and brightest, like Daniel and his friends, to Babylon to be trained to serve the empire. These captives would learn the values and beliefs of the dominant culture by studying "the language and literature of the Babylonians" (v. 4). Such texts included the history and accumulated wisdom of ancient Mesopotamia, going back to the time of the Sumerians.

In every way it seemed that evil prevailed in Daniel's new world. The Babylonians mocked the faith of his family by stripping treasures from the temple in Jerusalem and placing them in a Babylonian temple. This symbolized the triumph of Marduk, the patron god of Babylon, over the God of Israel. The Babylonians intended this to signal that the ancient faith of Israel had become irrelevant. In addition, their captors wined and dined Daniel and his friends with the best food available, the same fare served at "the king's table" (v. 5). They also gave them Babylonian names to indicate assimilation to the new environment. All traces of Israelite culture and faith had seemingly been removed.

Did You Know?
The endings of Daniel and his friend's names (-el and -iah) identified them with Israel's God. But the Babylonian names referenced Babylonian gods. Meshach, for example, means "Who is like Aku (the Babylonian moon god)."

The surrounding culture often seeks to draw us away from our identity in Christ. Jesus knew that His followers must remain in the world, but He told them not to be "of the world" (John 17:15-16). They must live among those who are unfriendly to His kingdom, but not be shaped by them. That is the challenge for every believer in every generation.

THE CULTURE CONFRONTATION

Daniel 1:8-10

Though surrounded by ungodly influences, Daniel did not forget his heritage or his faith. In fact, he held more tightly to them in this challenging environment. He "resolved not to defile himself with the royal food and wine" (v. 8). The term "defile" refers to something or someone becoming unfit for God, like a defective sacrifice or immoral person. Daniel felt the royal food would cause him to become unacceptable to God and he decided that could not happen.

Daniel does not explain exactly why the royal food defiled him. It may have been unclean according to Mosaic laws or perhaps offered to Babylonian gods prior to being served at the king's table. Whatever caused the food to defile him does not matter so much. The main point is that he realized it would compromise his relationship with God.

Standing against the current of Babylonian culture would not be easy. It involved considerable risk. He could literally lose his head and cause his superior the same fate. The king might just decide to eliminate them both for going contrary to established protocol. But God provided Daniel opportunity to be faithful: "God caused the official to show favor and sympathy" to him (v. 9). God made a way for Daniel to negotiate an alternative plan that would allow him to maintain his faith. Instead of eating the royal food, Daniel proposed eating only vegetables and drinking water for ten days (v. 12). If his health failed, then the authorities could do with him as they liked. In any case, he would not jeopardize his relationship with God.

Think About It

Babylonian literature contained the best collection of human knowledge available in the ancient world. Though mixed with pagan values, it enabled Daniel to understand the dominant culture and know when to challenge it.

As the world pushes us toward evil, God opens doors toward good. By God's grace we will find a means to do what is right in the most decadent circumstances. God will "provide a way out so that you can stand" against the temptations of this world (1 Corinthians 10:13).

THE CULTURE TRANSFORMATION

Daniel 1:17-20

God not only provided a way for Daniel to remain true to his convictions, God also gifted him and his friends with excellent health and superior "knowledge and understanding" (v. 17). After ten days of eating other food, Daniel and his friends "looked healthier and better nourished than any of the young men who ate the royal food" (v. 15). Later, after three years of training, the king examined them and found them "ten times better" than any of the wise men in the kingdom (v. 20). God rewarded the risk these young men took to remain committed to him.

Through this first story, Daniel helps believers see how they can live in the midst of ungodly cultures. At times, Daniel adopted some of the best things from the surrounding culture like its language and literature. He even accepted some of its benign customs such as names that were familiar to his captors.

It is clear, however, that Daniel took a stand when a cultural practice threatened his relationship with God. This confrontation came with considerable risk to himself and those around him. But in the end, God enabled Daniel and his friends to stand firm. As a result, they became transforming agents in the culture.

REFLECT

In what ways can you live each day with an "in the world, not of it" mentality?

JIM EDLIN is retired professor of Old Testament at MidAmerica Nazarene University.

SEEKING WISDOM FOR LIFE

Only God can give us the true wisdom we need for living today and into the future.

THE WORD

DANIEL 2:1-11

In the second year of his reign, Nebuchadnezzar had dreams; his
mind was troubled and he could not sleep. 2So the king summoned
the magicians, enchanters, sorcerers and astrologers to tell him what
he had dreamed. When they came in and stood before the king, 3he
said to them, "I have had a dream that troubles me and I want to
know what it means."

4Then the astrologers answered the king, "May the king live
forever! Tell your servants the dream, and we will interpret it."

5The king replied to the astrologers, "This is what I have firmly
decided: If you do not tell me what my dream was and interpret it,
I will have you cut into pieces and your houses turned into piles of
rubble. 6But if you tell me the dream and explain it, you will receive
from me gifts and rewards and great honor. So tell me the dream and
interpret it for me."

7Once more they replied, "Let the king tell his servants the
dream, and we will interpret it."

8Then the king answered, "I am certain that you are trying to gain
time, because you realize that this is what I have firmly decided: 9If
you do not tell me the dream, there is only one penalty for you. You
have conspired to tell me misleading and wicked things, hoping the
situation will change. So then, tell me the dream, and I will know that
you can interpret it for me."

10The astrologers answered the king, "There is no one on earth
who can do what the king asks! No king, however great and mighty,
has ever asked such a thing of any magician or enchanter or astrol-

oger. [11]What the king asks is too difficult. No one can reveal it to the
king except the gods, and they do not live among humans."

17-28a [17]Then Daniel returned to his house and explained the matter to
his friends Hananiah, Mishael and Azariah. [18]He urged them to plead
for mercy from the God of heaven concerning this mystery, so that he
and his friends might not be executed with the rest of the wise men
of Babylon. [19]During the night the mystery was revealed to Daniel in a
KEY VERSES vision. Then Daniel praised the God of heaven [20]and said: **"Praise be
to the name of God for ever and ever; wisdom and power are his.**
**[21]He changes times and seasons; he deposes kings and
raises up others. He gives wisdom to the wise and knowledge to
the discerning.**
[22]He reveals deep and hidden things; he knows what lies in dark-
ness, and light dwells with him.
[23]I thank and praise you, God of my ancestors: You have given me
wisdom and power, you have made known to me what we asked of
you, you have made known to us the dream of the king."
[24]Then Daniel went to Arioch, whom the king had appointed to
execute the wise men of Babylon, and said to him, "Do not execute
the wise men of Babylon. Take me to the king, and I will interpret his
dream for him."
[25]Arioch took Daniel to the king at once and said, "I have found
a man among the exiles from Judah who can tell the king what his
dream means."
[26]The king asked Daniel (also called Belteshazzar), "Are you able
to tell me what I saw in my dream and interpret it?"
[27]Daniel replied, "No wise man, enchanter, magician or diviner
can explain to the king the mystery he has asked about, [28]but there is
a God in heaven who reveals mysteries. He has shown King Nebuchadnezzar what will happen in days to come.

ENGAGE THE WORD

A KING NEEDS WISDOM

Daniel 2:1-11

King Nebuchadnezzar needed wisdom to interpret a dream. He had dreamed something that did not make sense and deeply troubled him. Like many people in the ancient world, the king believed the gods communicated with people through dreams. He also

Did You Know?

Biblical wisdom includes understanding how the world works and where life choices may take us. Knowing this enables a person to do the right thing at the right time in the right way.

knew that such dreams frequently carried foreboding messages.

So, Nebuchadnezzar called upon his most skilled interpreters, "the magicians, enchanters, sorcerers and astrologers" (v. 2). Each of these possessed particular abilities deemed useful for decoding communication from the divine realm. Some of them had studied records of past dreams. Others analyzed animal entrails or relied on ecstatic experiences to gain insight. Still others studied the movement of stars for clues. Once these experts determined the heavenly message, they devised incantations and potions to ward off its evil effects.

Normally, Babylonian wise men began with the content of a dream. Then they could suggest possible interpretations as well as remedies for its consequences. But Nebuchadnezzar refused to tell his wise men what was in the dream. He thought they should be able to do that.

Nebuchadnezzar expected far too much from human wisdom. The Babylonian wise men cconfessed: "There is no one on earth who can do what the king asks ... no one can reveal it to the king except the gods" (vv. 10-11). Even they knew only the divine could interpret the dream.

GOD REVEALS WISDOM

Daniel 2:17-23

Daniel's answer to finding wisdom was to turn to God. So, Daniel and his friends prayed earnestly for God to reveal the meaning of "this mystery" (v. 18). The word "mystery" refers to something that is secret or unknown to humans. By calling the dream a mystery they affirmed the same thing that their Babylonian colleagues had confessed. Their understanding was not adequate. They needed insight only God could provide.

Daniel understood that if God revealed the meaning of this mystery it would be because of God's "mercy" (v. 18). He knew that God is under no obligation to

Think About It
Even though God revealed the meaning of the king's dream to Daniel, people have continued to debate its details for centuries. Its main message remains clear, however: God overrules the rulers of this world.

share divine insight with humans. When He does, it is neither expected nor merited. God reveals wisdom out of the goodness of His heart.

Somewhere in the night, God "made known" to Daniel what the king had dreamed and what it meant (v. 23). In response, Daniel sang a song of praise that honored God for giving "wisdom to the wise" (v. 21). According to Proverbs 9:10, "the wise" are those who fear the Lord, like Daniel and his friends. They look to God for understanding and insight because true wisdom resides with God alone.

DANIEL SHARES WISDOM

Daniel 2:24-28a

When Daniel stood before King Nebuchadnezzar, he affirmed once more what Babylon's wise men had confessed. He could not know the meaning of the king's dream using his own skills. He admitted, "No wise man ... can explain to the king the mystery" (v. 27). However, he went on to say, "There is a God in heaven who reveals mysteries" (v. 28). God knows what humans do not know and chooses to share it as He wills.

Daniel explained the king's dream because God graciously revealed it to him. The dream was about an enormous statue of precious metals being crushed by a rock. Its images were stunning as well as puzzling. Its message, however, was not complicated. Simply put, the dream proclaimed that though earthly kingdoms appear impressive and strong, God's kingdom overcomes them all. Such truth is wisdom for life in any generation. It encourages people who belong to God and warns those who do not. God's people can be courageous and remain steadfast, because God wins in the end.

REFLECT In what ways do you need God's wisdom today?

JIM EDLIN

LIVING IN THE FIRE

When circumstances are against us, the Lord stands beside us.

THE WORD

DANIEL 3:8-20

At this time some astrologers came forward and denounced the Jews. 9They said to King Nebuchadnezzar, "May the king live forever! 10Your Majesty has issued a decree that everyone who hears the sound of the horn, flute, zither, lyre, harp, pipe and all kinds of music must fall down and worship the image of gold, 11and that whoever does not fall down and worship will be thrown into a blazing furnace. 12But there are some Jews whom you have set over the affairs of the province of Babylon—Shadrach, Meshach and Abednego—who pay no attention to you, Your Majesty. They neither serve your gods nor worship the image of gold you have set up."

13Furious with rage, Nebuchadnezzar summoned Shadrach, Meshach and Abednego. So these men were brought before the king, 14and Nebuchadnezzar said to them, "Is it true, Shadrach, Meshach and Abednego, that you do not serve my gods or worship the image of gold I have set up? 15Now when you hear the sound of the horn, flute, zither, lyre, harp, pipe and all kinds of music, if you are ready to fall down and worship the image I made, very good. But if you do not worship it, you will be thrown immediately into a blazing furnace. Then what god will be able to rescue you from my hand?"

16Shadrach, Meshach and Abednego replied to him, "King Nebuchadnezzar, we do not need to defend ourselves before you in this matter. **17If we are thrown into the blazing furnace, the God we serve is able to deliver us from it, and he will deliver us from Your Majesty's hand. 18But even if he does not, we want you to know, Your Majesty, that we will not serve your gods or worship the image of gold you have set up."**

KEY VERSES

[19]Then Nebuchadnezzar was furious with Shadrach, Meshach
and Abednego, and his attitude toward them changed. He ordered
the furnace heated seven times hotter than usual [20]and commanded
some of the strongest soldiers in his army to tie up Shadrach, Meshach and Abednego and throw them into the blazing furnace.

24-26 [24]Then King Nebuchadnezzar leaped to his feet in amazement
and asked his advisers, "Weren't there three men that we tied up and
threw into the fire?"
They replied, "Certainly, Your Majesty."
[25]He said, "Look! I see four men walking around in the fire, unbound and unharmed, and the fourth looks like a son of the gods."
[26]Nebuchadnezzar then approached the opening of the blazing
furnace and shouted, "Shadrach, Meshach and Abednego, servants of
the Most High God, come out! Come here!"
So Shadrach, Meshach and Abednego came out of the fire.

ENGAGE THE WORD

THE DILEMMA

Daniel 3:8-15

King Nebuchadnezzar did not learn much from his dream in chapter 2. He continued to imagine that he ruled the world rather than God. As a result, he set up an impressive golden image and invited everyone in his kingdom to its dedication. Whether the image was a likeness of himself, one of his gods, or something else, we are not told. In any case, it represented his grandeur and might.

At the dedication ceremony, Nebuchadnezzar offered two options to his subjects: bow or burn. He decreed that everyone must "fall down and worship the image of gold" when music played (v. 9). Anyone who did not bow down would be "thrown into a blazing furnace" (v. 11). This decree included everyone, all "peoples, nations and men of every language" according to verse 4. No one was excluded.

"Some astrologers" (v. 8) revealed their prejudice and jealousy when they reported Shadrach, Meshach, and Abednego to the king. They describe their co-workers as "Jews whom you have set over the affairs

Did You Know?
Today's story contains humor in the way it mocks Babylonian worship. The long list of musical instruments ridicules the futility of pompous worship designed to get the attention of preoccupied, unsympathetic gods of Babylon.

THE DECISION

of the province of Babylon" (v. 12). They might have added, "instead of us." Those foreigners had the jobs that they wanted.

When Nebuchadnezzar learned of the stance that Shadrach, Meshach, and Abednego had taken, he became "furious with rage" (v. 13). He apparently felt disrespected. Godly people often upset arrogant people of this world. So, when the king pronounced his ultimatum once again, he finished with a taunt. He mockingly asked, "Then what god will be able to rescue you from my hand?" (v. 15).

Daniel 3:16-20

Though Nebuchadnezzar may have intended his question as rhetorical, Shadrach, Meshach, and Abednego responded as if he had asked for an answer. They declared, "the God we serve is able to save us" and "will rescue us from your hand" (v. 17). They believed God fully capable of overcoming any threat that this world might throw at them. But they left the outcome in God's hands. They did not presume to tell God what to do. If God chose not to rescue them, they would still hold fast to their convictions. They would not break God's commandments and "serve your gods" or "worship the image of gold" (v. 18). God had put these laws first in the list of Ten Commandments for a reason. That is where a committed relationship to God begins.

Shadrach, Meshach, and Abednego firmly decided to go with God rather than the crowd. Intimidation from peers and the most powerful man in the world did not alter their decision. There was no room for discussion. They did "not need to defend" their actions, because they were guilty as charged (v. 16). They had chosen God's way, not the way of the world.

Such conviction is very admirable. But it does not always gain the respect of the world. In the case of Shadrach, Meshach, and Abednego, it intensified the fury of the king and the heat of the furnace at the same time. In the end, their faith in God got them thrown into the fire.

Think About It
Nebuchadnezzar constructed an idol to promote himself. But in the end, this provided a means to display God's greatness. We might wonder what other means God could use to reveal himself in this world.

THE DELIVERANCE

Daniel 3:24-26

God may not have rescued his servants from being thrown into the fire. But He did protect them in the midst of it and eventually delivered them from it. Nebuchadnezzar and his advisers witnessed this first-hand. They saw the three Jewish men "walking around in the fire, unbound and unharmed" (v. 25). This is remarkable since the soldiers who carried out the execution died from the heat. Surviving the furnace was impossible. But God overcame the impossible.

Further, the king observed another person with them who looked "like a son of the gods" (v. 25). Whether this was an angel, as the king noted later in verse 28, or perhaps even Jesus before His birth, we cannot say for certain. What remains important is that God came alongside His committed servants in their distress. God went with His faithful followers into the fire. Those who stood up for God did not stand alone.

In the end, the king who ordered the execution reversed it. He invited Shadrach, Meshach, and Abednego to "come out" of the furnace (v. 26). Then, he acknowledged that the God of these men must be "the Most High God" (v. 26). For Nebuchadnezzar, this meant that the Jewish God headed up the pantheon of gods in his world. He was partly right. Though there is no collection of other gods, the God of Shadrach, Meshach, and Abednego is greater than any divine power one might imagine. This God goes into the furnace with those who chose to go against the crowd and stand for Him.

REFLECT Is there a fiery situation from which you need God's rescue?

JIM EDLIN

THE SIN OF ARROGANCE

God holds people accountable for their arrogance.

THE WORD

DANIEL 5:1-5 King Belshazzar gave a great banquet for a thousand of his nobles
and drank wine with them. [2]While Belshazzar was drinking his
wine, he gave orders to bring in the gold and silver goblets that Nebuchadnezzar his father had taken from the temple in Jerusalem, so that
the king and his nobles, his wives and his concubines might drink from
them. [3]So they brought in the gold goblets that had been taken from
the temple of God in Jerusalem, and the king and his nobles, his wives
and his concubines drank from them. [4]As they drank the wine, they
praised the gods of gold and silver, of bronze, iron, wood and stone.
[5]Suddenly the fingers of a human hand appeared and wrote on
the plaster of the wall, near the lampstand in the royal palace. The
king watched the hand as it wrote.

8-9 [8]Then all the king's wise men came in, but they could not read the
writing or tell the king what it meant. [9]So King Belshazzar became even
more terrified and his face grew more pale. His nobles were baffled.

17-30 [17]Then Daniel answered the king, "You may keep your gifts for
yourself and give your rewards to someone else. Nevertheless, I will
read the writing for the king and tell him what it means.
[18]"Your Majesty, the Most High God gave your father Nebuchadnezzar sovereignty and greatness and glory and splendor. [19]Because of the
high position he gave him, all the nations and peoples of every language
dreaded and feared him. Those the king wanted to put to death, he put to
death; those he wanted to spare, he spared; those he wanted to promote,

he promoted; and those he wanted to humble, he humbled. [20]But when
his heart became arrogant and hardened with pride, he was deposed
from his royal throne and stripped of his glory. [21]He was driven away from
people and given the mind of an animal; he lived with the wild donkeys
and ate grass like the ox; and his body was drenched with the dew of
heaven, until he acknowledged that the Most High God is sovereign over
all kingdoms on earth and sets over them anyone he wishes.

KEY VERSES

**[22]"But you, Belshazzar, his son, have not humbled yourself,
though you knew all this. [23]Instead, you have set yourself up
against the Lord of heaven. You had the goblets from his temple
brought to you, and you and your nobles, your wives and your
concubines drank wine from them. You praised the gods of silver
and gold, of bronze, iron, wood and stone, which cannot see or
hear or understand. But you did not honor the God who holds in
his hand your life and all your ways.** [24]Therefore he sent the hand
that wrote the inscription.

[25]"This is the inscription that was written: mene, mene, tekel, parsin

[26]"Here is what these words mean: Mene: God has numbered the
days of your reign and brought it to an end.

[27]Tekel: You have been weighed on the scales and found wanting.

[28]Peres: Your kingdom is divided and given to the Medes and
Persians."

[29]Then at Belshazzar's command, Daniel was clothed in purple,
a gold chain was placed around his neck, and he was proclaimed the
third highest ruler in the kingdom.

[30]That very night Belshazzar, king of the Babylonians, was slain.

ENGAGE THE WORD

ARROGANCE DISPLAYED

Daniel 5:1-4

Belshazzar wanted to impress the leaders of his realm. So, he put on a great banquet, surrounded himself with thousands of the nation's leading citizens, and let wine flow freely. All this likely took place in the massive throne room hall of "the royal palace" complex in Babylon (v. 5).

In order to accentuate his importance further, Belshazzar ordered "gold and silver goblets" be used for drinking wine (v. 2). These were no ordinary goblets however. They came from the plunder of the

> **Did You Know?**
> Babylonian records never officially designated Belshazzar as king. His father, Nabonidus, was the ruling monarch and only placed his son in authority during his absence from the city of Babylon.

Jewish temple in Jerusalem during the days of his predecessor Nebuchadnezzar. Drinking from them not only underscored the dominating reach of Babylonian empire, it also expressed contempt for the God of the Jews. Belshazzar flaunted a fearless disregard for God. To push the point further, he used the goblets to toast the images of gods collected from other conquests. Ironically, some of these idols were made of the same material as the goblets.

By the world's standards, Belshazzar appeared to have much to boast about. He seemed to wield great power, possess vast resources, and attract many friends. In addition, he showed no fear of offending the divine realms. All of this, however, was misplaced pride of a petty person.

ARROGANCE CHALLENGED

Daniel 5:5, 8-9

God disrupted Belshazzar's self-promoting party in a startling manner. A disembodied "human hand appeared and wrote on the plaster of the wall" (v. 5). Such a sight captured everyone's attention, especially the king's. His brazen arrogance quickly disappeared and his pretentious shell of confidence dissolved. The entire banquet had been a show and Belshazzar knew it. According to ancient historians, he likely knew that Persian armies were within a few miles of Babylon. They had captured key cities and were marching toward the capitol to complete the conquest.

Knowing this made the message on the wall all the more unsettling to the king. Yet, none of his wise men could read it let alone "tell the king what it meant" (v. 8). Babylon's best diviners failed to understand what God was saying. They were skilled in hearing other voices, but not God's. The words of God made no sense to those unaccustomed to hearing Him speak.

ARROGANCE EXPOSED

Daniel 5:17-30

Belshazzar's only hope of understanding God's words to him came through a man who was in touch

Think About It

In the end, both Daniel and Belshazzar received their just rewards. Daniel was promoted for his humility and wisdom, while Belshazzar was demoted for his arrogance and ignorance.

with God, Daniel. The message, as the king suspected, was not encouraging.

Before interpreting the wall writing though, Daniel began with a history lesson. He recapped the story recorded in Daniel 4 about Belshazzar's most famous predecessor Nebuchadnezzar. He had flaunted his power too. But God humbled him "until he acknowledged that the Most High God is sovereign" (5:21). This highlighted a crucial difference between the two kings. Nebuchadnezzar eventually submitted to the authority of God, but Belshazzar had "not humbled" himself (v. 22). In an effort to impress people Belshazzar had set himself "up against the Lord of heaven" (v. 23).

Belshazzar acted as if he answered to no one. But, in fact, he did. Daniel told him that the God he refused to honor actually "holds in his hands your life" (v. 23). The king of Babylon was accountable to One greater than himself. God would assess his life and administer justice. This was the message of the four words on the wall. Belshazzar's actions and attitudes had been "weighed" *(Tekel)* on God's scales of justice and not measured up (v. 27). Therefore, God had "numbered" *(Mene)* the days that the king would reign (5:26). He would sit on the throne only as long as God decided. Then, the Babylonian kingdom would come to an end. It would be "divided" *(Peres)* and conquered by their enemies the Medes and the Persians (5:28).

God's message found immediate fulfillment as "that very night Belshazzar...was slain and Darius the Mede took over the kingdom" (5:30). The trap of arrogance snared another pompous pretender, while God continued to rule over heaven and earth.

REFLECT Pray, asking God to show you any areas of your life where arrogant attitudes might have crept in?

JIM EDLIN

REMAINING FAITHFUL TO GOD

Our faithful lives speak as loudly as our faithful words.

THE WORD

DANIEL 6:3-10

Now Daniel so distinguished himself among the administrators and
the satraps by his exceptional qualities that the king planned to
set him over the whole kingdom. 4At this, the administrators and the
satraps tried to find grounds for charges against Daniel in his conduct
of government affairs, but they were unable to do so. They could find
no corruption in him, because he was trustworthy and neither corrupt
nor negligent. 5Finally these men said, "We will never find any basis
for charges against this man Daniel unless it has something to do
with the law of his God."

6So these administrators and satraps went as a group to the king
and said: "May King Darius live forever! 7The royal administrators,
prefects, satraps, advisers and governors have all agreed that the
king should issue an edict and enforce the decree that anyone who
prays to any god or human being during the next thirty days, except
to you, Your Majesty, shall be thrown into the lions' den. 8Now, Your
Majesty, issue the decree and put it in writing so that it cannot be al-
tered—in accordance with the law of the Medes and Persians, which
cannot be repealed." 9So King Darius put the decree in writing.

KEY VERSE

**10Now when Daniel learned that the decree had been published,
he went home to his upstairs room where the windows opened
toward Jerusalem. Three times a day he got down on his knees and
prayed, giving thanks to his God, just as he had done before.**

15-16

15Then the men went as a group to King Darius and said to him,
"Remember, Your Majesty, that according to the law of the Medes and
Persians no decree or edict that the king issues can be changed."

[16]So the king gave the order, and they brought Daniel and threw
him into the lions' den. The king said to Daniel, "May your God, whom
you serve continually, rescue you!"

19-23 [19]At the first light of dawn, the king got up and hurried to the
lions' den. [20]When he came near the den, he called to Daniel in an an-
guished voice, "Daniel, servant of the living God, has your God, whom
you serve continually, been able to rescue you from the lions?"
[21]Daniel answered, "May the king live forever! [22]My God sent his
angel, and he shut the mouths of the lions. They have not hurt me,
because I was found innocent in his sight. Nor have I ever done any
wrong before you, Your Majesty."
[23]The king was overjoyed and gave orders to lift Daniel out of the
den. And when Daniel was lifted from the den, no wound was found
on him, because he had trusted in his God.

ENGAGE THE WORD

FAITH OBSERVED

Daniel 6:3-5

Daniel's conduct spoke volumes to his contemporaries. He lived such an exemplary life that the king of Persia as well as his coworkers took notice. They observed his "exceptional qualities" (literally his "excellent spirit"), which included being "trustworthy and neither corrupt nor negligent" (vv. 3-4). That is to say, he did not deviate from his basic principles and could not be bought off. He remained diligently committed to his duties. These qualities made him the kind of person the king wanted administering his affairs. As a result, he planned to promote Daniel to a high position.

Not everyone was pleased with Daniel's good qualities however. These characteristics caused his fellow (jealous) administrators to look for a way to bring him down. The only thing they could find was "something to do with the law of his God" (v. 5), which they had noticed he followed closely. Surely these laws would come into conflict with the laws of the state. They were right, of course. The goals of the human institutions often differ from God's goals.

Unfortunately, those who follow the Lord are not

Did You Know?
The Persians developed one of the best organized empires the world has ever seen. The satrap system of administration reflected in this story allowed it to continue for over 200 years.

FAITH CHALLENGED

admired by everyone. Some people feel threatened when they see others live to please God. Jesus experienced this firsthand and warned His disciples, "If the world hates you, keep in mind that it hated me first" (John 15:18). When people notice that God's ways are not their ways, they often resent it.

Daniel 6:6-10

Daniel's enemies devised an ingenious plan to do away with him. They appealed to the king's sense of self-importance and proposed that all prayers to gods be directed through him for a month. Since Persian kings did not think of themselves as being divine, the point was that the king would become the sole mediator between heaven and earth. Those who did not submit to this decree would meet certain death in a den of hungry lions.

This set up a challenge between the law of Daniel's God and "the law of the Medes and Persians" (v. 8). The law by which Daniel lived stated that there should be "no other gods before" the Lord (Exodus 20:3). The law of the Persians called for acknowledging and submitting to all kinds of gods. The two laws came into direct conflict. If one were followed, the other would be broken.

Daniel chose to follow the law of his God and continued to do what he had been in the habit of doing: "He got down on his knees and prayed, giving thanks to his God" (v. 10). Though his decision to violate Persian law could not have been easy, his consistent discipline of daily prayer must have been less difficult. Daniel had "learned that the decree had been published" and understood what that meant (v. 10). He knew the consequences. But his spiritual discipline held him steady when the world challenged his beliefs.

Interestingly, we are told that Daniel was "giving thanks to his God" in his prayer time (v. 10). What could he possibly be thankful for? Was he thankful that God would be with him in this ordeal? Was

Think About It

The only time Daniel speaks in this story is in the lion's den. His actions communicated more about his faith than his words. Both the king and his accusers clearly saw his beliefs in how he lived.

he thankful for an opportunity to witness for God through this circumstance? Whatever Daniel may have been thinking, he does not say. We only know what he did. He continued to talk with God and give thanks.

FAITH REWARDED

Daniel 6:15-16, 19-23

Daniel's enemies noticed his defiance of the Persian edict and immediately reported it to the king. However, the king did not move quickly. Instead of being angry, he looked for a way to save Daniel because he knew his value. But, in the end, he could not rescue him. The law designed to exalt the king actually ended up oppressing him. Even the king could not overturn his own law.

Humanly speaking, Daniel had no chance of surviving a den of lions. Yet, the king expressed some hope when he called out to Daniel, "May your God, whom you serve continually, rescue you" (v. 16). Was this wishful thinking or an earnest prayer? Whatever his intent, the king received his answer early the next morning. He called into the pit and heard Daniel respond, "My God sent his angel and shut the mouths of the lions" (v. 22). When the Persians closed the mouth of the den, the Lord closed the mouths of the lions.

Daniel emerged from the pit of certain death without a scratch. "He had trusted in his God" and God came through (v. 23). The story never indicates that he expected to be delivered. He simply remained faithful and trusted that God ruled regardless of circumstances. As a result, the king observed that Daniel's God was "the living God," not a dead or distracted god (v. 20). Daniel's God actually responded to people and made a difference in their lives. The truth of God's goodness became evident to the world through the faithful actions of his servant.

REFLECT

Are you currently in a "lion's den"? If so, in what ways can your life be an expression of your faithfulness toward God?

JIM EDLIN

DEALING WITH EVIL KINGDOMS

Though earthly kingdoms rise and fall, God continues to reign over His world.

THE WORD

DANIEL 7:2-9

Daniel said: "In my vision at night I looked, and there before me were the four winds of heaven churning up the great sea. [3]Four great beasts, each different from the others, came up out of the sea.

[4]"The first was like a lion, and it had the wings of an eagle. I watched until its wings were torn off and it was lifted from the ground so that it stood on two feet like a human being, and the mind of a human was given to it.

[5]"And there before me was a second beast, which looked like a bear. It was raised up on one of its sides, and it had three ribs in its mouth between its teeth. It was told, 'Get up and eat your fill of flesh!'

[6]"After that, I looked, and there before me was another beast, one that looked like a leopard. And on its back it had four wings like those of a bird. This beast had four heads, and it was given authority to rule.

[7]"After that, in my vision at night I looked, and there before me was a fourth beast—terrifying and frightening and very powerful. It had large iron teeth; it crushed and devoured its victims and trampled underfoot whatever was left. It was different from all the former beasts, and it had ten horns.

[8]"While I was thinking about the horns, there before me was another horn, a little one, which came up among them; and three of the first horns were uprooted before it. This horn had eyes like the eyes of a human being and a mouth that spoke boastfully.

[9]"As I looked, "thrones were set in place, and the Ancient of Days took his seat. His clothing was as white as snow; the hair of his head was white like wool. His throne was flaming with fire, and its wheels were all ablaze.

11-14 [11]"Then I continued to watch because of the boastful words the
horn was speaking. I kept looking until the beast was slain and its
body destroyed and thrown into the blazing fire. [12](The other beasts
had been stripped of their authority, but were allowed to live for a
period of time.)
[13]"In my vision at night I looked, and there before me was one
like a son of man, coming with the clouds of heaven. He approached
KEY VERSE the Ancient of Days and was led into his presence. **[14]He was given
authority, glory and sovereign power; all nations and peoples of
every language worshiped him. His dominion is an everlasting
dominion that will not pass away, and his kingdom is one that
will never be destroyed.**

ENGAGE THE WORD

THE CHAOS OF EVIL KINGDOMS

Daniel 7:2-8

God gave Daniel a glimpse of what earthly kingdoms look like from heaven's perspective. With dramatic images, Daniel's vision portrays the kingdoms of this world as brutally destructive and terrifying. Each one emerges from the windswept, chaotic waters of the ocean displaying its own special brand of power and terror. The three most feared wild beasts represent the first three kingdoms: a lion, a bear, and a leopard. Each is malformed in some way to intensify its terror. The fourth beast cannot compare to anything in this world because it is even more horrifying than the first three. This kingdom ruthlessly "crushed and devoured its victims and trampled underfoot whatever was left" (v. 7). Its many "horns" seem to signify its different rulers, who rise and fall just like the kingdom over which they rule (v. 8).

Whether these beasts were meant to symbolize particular nations or all earthly kingdoms in general, they relate important messages as a group. First, we see that human governments tend to oppress rather than empower people. They exploit, devour, and crush their subjects. Further, as one realm replaces another, they become increasingly frightening and oppressive.

Did You Know?

The visions in the latter part of Daniel reaffirm the stories in the first part. Together they assure God's people that God remains fully in control of this world both now and into the future.

THE JUSTICE OF GOD'S KINGDOM

Rather than improve they decline. Such a picture of human governance should not surprise us however. Power in the hands of sinful people always leads to disaster. We have witnessed it over and over again throughout world history. Without God human institutions always generate confusion, eventually destroy the beautiful world God intended, and ultimately fail.

Daniel 7:9, 11-12

With verse 9 the scene changes abruptly from chaos to calm. The justness of God's benevolent rule contrasts sharply with the horror of human governance. God comes to judge the kingdoms of this world sitting upon a throne as the unquestioned Ruler over all. He is called "the Ancient of Days" to underscore the long-standing authority by which He rules humankind (v. 9). God has been there from the beginning and even before any earthly kingdom. His white clothing and hair, along with "his throne ... flaming with fire and its wheels ... all ablaze," add to the impression of God's sovereign control and right to judge humanity (v. 9).

Each beast of earth submits to God's judgment. The most threatening beast, the fourth one, is "slain and its body destroyed" (v. 11). All its evil power is erased. The other three beasts are "stripped of their authority" so that they no longer threaten people (v. 12). Those who devoured others are consumed by God's inescapable judgment.

At this point, Daniel caught a vision of what God has done and promises to do throughout the Bible. As Isaiah explained, when God is ready to do so, "the LORD will march out like a champion, like a warrior he will stir up his zeal; with a shout he will raise the battle cry and will triumph over his enemies" (Isaiah 42:13). God's passion for this world means He will not allow evil to triumph in it. He will bring down those who destroy His creation and cause chaos. Evil does not have the final word in God's world.

Think About It

Both chapter 2 and chapter 7 give dramatic images of earthly kingdoms. The impressive statue of chapter 2 views them from a human perspective, while the terrifying beasts of chapter 7 sees them from God's.

THE BEAUTY OF GOD'S KINGDOM

Daniel 7:13-14

Following the judgment of the beasts, a beautiful scene emerges. God inaugurates a new ruler to govern a new kingdom in this world. In contrast to the kingdoms of the beasts, His kingdom "is an everlasting dominion that will not pass away" (v 14). While human realms always come to an end, this kingdom never does. Order and permanence mark this new kingdom.

The new ruler of God's kingdom is described as "one like a son of man, coming on the clouds of heaven" (v. 13). This is exactly how Jesus described himself in Matthew 24:30. In addition, Jesus regularly referred to himself as "the Son of Man" throughout His life on earth. In this way He identified himself with the one Daniel envisioned in this passage. Though He was human (a son of man), He was also divine (coming on the clouds of heaven). As a result, "all nations and peoples of every language worshiped him" (v. 14).

Jesus proclaimed the fulfillment of Daniel's vision when He preached that "the kingdom of heaven has come near" (Matthew 4:17). The kingdom envisioned by Daniel became reality in Jesus and only awaited His second coming to appear in all its fullness. The kingdom that "will never be destroyed" arrived among us when Jesus came to earth (v. 14).

This vision encouraged people in Daniel's world not to be overly concerned about evil human kingdoms, whether Babylonian, Persian, or some other entity. Those kingdoms would eventually fall. God would judge them and someday remove them from this world. The same is true for us today, yet even more so. God's kingdom has already come into our world. Jesus reigns now and His kingdom will never end.

REFLECT Today, thank God for being the Ruler over heaven and earth.

JIM EDLIN

A REPENTANT PROPHET AND A RESPONSIVE GOD

We can intercede on behalf of our Christian communities for the good of God's kingdom.

THE WORD

DANIEL 9:1-9

In the first year of Darius son of Xerxes (a Mede by descent), who
was made ruler over the Babylonian kingdom—[2]in the first year of
his reign, I, Daniel, understood from the Scriptures, according to the
word of the LORD given to Jeremiah the prophet, that the desolation of
Jerusalem would last seventy years. [3]So I turned to the LORD God and
pleaded with him in prayer and petition, in fasting, and in sackcloth
and ashes.

[4]I prayed to the LORD my God and confessed:

"LORD, the great and awesome God, who keeps his covenant of
love with those who love him and keep his commandments, [5]we have
sinned and done wrong. We have been wicked and have rebelled;
we have turned away from your commands and laws. [6]We have not
listened to your servants the prophets, who spoke in your name to our
kings, our princes and our ancestors, and to all the people of the land.

[7]"LORD, you are righteous, but this day we are covered with
shame—the people of Judah and the inhabitants of Jerusalem and all
Israel, both near and far, in all the countries where you have scattered
us because of our unfaithfulness to you. [8]We and our kings, our princes and our ancestors are covered with shame, LORD, because we have
sinned against you. [9]The LORD our God is merciful and forgiving, even
though we have rebelled against him;

17-19

[17]"Now, our God, hear the prayers and petitions of your servant.
For your sake, LORD, look with favor on your desolate sanctuary. [18]Give
ear, our God, and hear; open your eyes and see the desolation of the
city that bears your Name. We do not make requests of you because

we are righteous, but because of your great mercy. [19]Lord, listen!
Lord, forgive! Lord, hear and act! For your sake, my God, do not delay,
because your city and your people bear your Name."

21-24 [21]while I was still in prayer, Gabriel, the man I had seen in the
earlier vision, came to me in swift flight about the time of the evening
sacrifice. [22]He instructed me and said to me, "Daniel, I have now
KEY VERSES come to give you insight and understanding. **[23]As soon as you began
to pray, a word went out, which I have come to tell you, for you
are highly esteemed. Therefore, consider the word and understand the vision:**
**[24]"Seventy 'sevens' are decreed for your people and your
holy city to finish transgression, to put an end to sin, to atone
for wickedness, to bring in everlasting righteousness, to seal up
vision and prophecy and to anoint the Most Holy Place.**

ENGAGE THE WORD

DANIEL'S CALL TO INTERCESSION

Daniel 9:1-3

Anytime is a good time to pray. But certain occasions call for more intense prayer than others. This was one of those times for Daniel. His reading of Jeremiah's prophecy had led to new understanding. Through Jeremiah, God had said that Judah would "serve the king of Babylon seventy years" and "when seventy years are completed for Babylon, I will come to you and ... bring you back to this place" (Jeremiah 25:11 and 29:10). Daniel noted that "the first year" of Persian rule in 539 BC had ended almost seventy years of Babylonian domination of Judah (v. 1). Perhaps it was time for God to fulfill His promise to Daniel's people.

The Babylonian conquest of Judah had been devastating for its people as well as for God's reputation. Jerusalem and its temple had been leveled to the ground. A large portion of Judah's population had been killed or displaced over the Middle East. Many, including Daniel, had been forced to live in exile in Babylon for generations. Because of this, people of the world viewed Israel's God as weak and irrelevant.

Did You Know?

Numbers in Daniel were symbolic and not meant to be calculated. Seventy is the perfect number times 10. It symbolizes a complete amount of time, like a full life in which a person might see several generations of descendants.

DANIEL'S PRAYER OF INTERCESSION

They dismissed testimonies of His compassion and grace as well as His claim to supremacy.

Realizing this crucial moment in Israel's history, when the fortunes of God and His people could change, Daniel sought the Lord earnestly. He fasted and put on mourning clothes of "sackcloth and ashes" to indicate his desperate desire for God's intervention (v. 3).

Daniel 9:4-9, 17-19

Daniel's prayer highlights the stark contrast between the awesomeness of God and the awfulness of sin. Throughout the prayer, the prophet addresses God as "Lord" *(adonai),* a name that affirms God's sovereign command over this world (v 4). He remains in full control of every part of creation regardless of what circumstances might suggest. God is especially "great and awesome" because He "keeps his covenant of love" with His people (v. 3). God graciously engaged Abraham and his descendants in a binding love relationship. This is why Daniel also addresses God as "our God" (vv. 9, 10, 13, 14, 15, 17, 18). He and his people belonged to God, and God belonged to them.

Throughout the centuries God had remained faithful to His commitment to the covenant even though Israel had not. Daniel confessed their unfaithfulness in every way he could think to say it. They have "sinned ... done wrong ... been wicked ... rebelled ... turned away" and "not listened" (vv. 5-6). That just about covers it all. As the first term "sinned" suggests, they missed God's best for their lives. As a result, they were "covered with shame" (v. 7). They had embarrassed themselves as well as God.

Daniel admitted that God was right to send His people into exile. That was only fair. But Daniel also knew that God was "merciful and forgiving" (v. 9). So, on this basis, he pleaded for God to "listen . . . forgive . . . hear and act" (v. 19). Though God was right to put His people in exile, God would also be right to show

Think About It

Israel's prophets found spiritual insight from reading the words of other prophets. In their messages, they frequently alluded to earlier prophets like Moses, Hosea, Isaiah, and Jeremiah.

mercy. That is also in keeping with who God is. He is the God of "great mercy" (v. 18).

GOD'S RESPONSE TO INTERCESSION

Daniel 9:21-24

Daniel received an immediate response from God. It was even delivered by an angel. However, the answer was not exactly what he wanted to hear nor as clear as he might have hoped it would be. Judgment for sin was not over and the day of full redemption remained somewhere in the future.

The details about the future were puzzling, but the main point of God's message was crystal clear. The angel explained that "seventy 'sevens' are decreed for your people" before God would restore His kingdom on earth (v. 24). That is to say, it would be a long time before things were set right again. The time when Daniel's people would "finish transgression" remained some time away (v. 24). As a result, the day of "everlasting righteousness" would be put off (v. 24). How long this would be is not clearly spelled out. "Seventy 'sevens'" simply conveyed an indefinite amount of time.

So, Daniel did not get all his questions answered, just like many of us have experienced. God did not give the prophet a blueprint of how the future might unfold. Yet, God did clarify what He desired from His people. God wanted them "to finish transgression" and "put an end to sin" (v 24). He was looking for a holy people, as He always has. .

The day of final and full salvation remains somewhere in the future. In the meantime, we can pray like Daniel for our friends and neighbors. We can ask God to make us holy people in preparation for the day when He finally rules supreme over this world and the day of "everlasting righteousness" finally dawns (v. 24).

REFLECT Who can you breathe an intercessory prayer for today?

JIM EDLIN

GOD WORKS BEHIND THE SCENES

Even when we cannot see it, God is working to accomplish His will in this world.

THE WORD

ESTHER 1:1-3 This is what happened during the time of Xerxes, the Xerxes who
ruled over 127 provinces stretching from India to Cush: [2]At that
time King Xerxes reigned from his royal throne in the citadel of Susa,
[3]and in the third year of his reign he gave a banquet for all his nobles
and officials. The military leaders of Persia and Media, the princes,
and the nobles of the provinces were present.

10-12 [10]On the seventh day, when King Xerxes was in high spirits from
wine, he commanded the seven eunuchs who served him—Me-
human, Biztha, Harbona, Bigtha, Abagtha, Zethar and Karkas—[11]to
bring before him Queen Vashti, wearing her royal crown, in order to
display her beauty to the people and nobles, for she was lovely to look
at. [12]But when the attendants delivered the king's command, Queen
Vashti refused to come. Then the king became furious and burned
with anger.

ESTHER 2:1-2 [1]Later when King Xerxes' fury had subsided, he remembered
Vashti and what she had done and what he had decreed about her.
[2]Then the king's personal attendants proposed, "Let a search be
made for beautiful young virgins for the king.

5-10 **[5]Now there was in the citadel of Susa a Jew of the tribe of**
KEY VERSES **Benjamin, named Mordecai son of Jair, the son of Shimei, the**
son of Kish, [6]who had been carried into exile from Jerusalem by
Nebuchadnezzar king of Babylon, among those taken captive
with Jehoiachin king of Judah. [7]Mordecai had a cousin named

Hadassah, whom he had brought up because she had neither father
nor mother. This young woman, who was also known as Esther, had
a lovely figure and was beautiful. Mordecai had taken her as his own
daughter when her father and mother died.

[8]When the king's order and edict had been proclaimed, many
young women were brought to the citadel of Susa and put under the
care of Hegai. Esther also was taken to the king's palace and entrusted to Hegai, who had charge of the harem. [9]She pleased him and won
his favor. Immediately he provided her with her beauty treatments and
special food. He assigned to her seven female attendants selected
from the king's palace and moved her and her attendants into the
best place in the harem.

[10]Esther had not revealed her nationality and family background,
because Mordecai had forbidden her to do so.

17 [17]Now the king was attracted to Esther more than to any of the
other women, and she won his favor and approval more than any of
the other virgins. So he set a royal crown on her head and made her
queen instead of Vashti.

ENGAGE THE WORD

A TIME WHEN PERSIANS RULED

Esther 1:1-3

The beginning of this story alerts the reader that the setting is during the reign of King Xerxes **(Heb. Ahasuerus),** a time when the Persians ruled over Judah. King Xerxes ruled from 486-465 BC. Esther 1:1 begins with the phrase "and it was in the days." This particular phrase is found in only four other places in the Old Testament: Genesis 14:1; Isaiah 7:1; Jeremiah 1:3; and Ruth 1:1. Most of the time this phrase is connected to a specific ruler, except in Ruth 1:1, which connects it to an era, "the days the judges ruled."

The opening scene also reveals a lavish banquet setting. Banquets (1:3, 5, 9; 2:18; 5:5; 7:1) and feasting (8:17; 9:17-22) are found throughout the story. Opulence is witnessed through references to cloth, clothing, and objects (see Esther 1:6-7), and are key items to pay attention to as they indicate shifts in power and markers of identity.

Did You Know?

One of the main accounts outside of the biblical text that describes the context of Esther is from the writings of Herodotus, a Greek historian, who wrote extensively about King Xerxes in *Histories of the Persians Wars* (490-480 BC). His writings should be read with a healthy dose of skepticism because of his Greek allegiance, but it is intriguing that about a third of his book details the reign of King Xerxes.

QUEEN VASHTI

Esther 1:10-12

Queen Vashti is hosting a banquet for the women while her husband is hosting a separate banquet. King Xerxes demands Queen Vashti to appear before him wearing her royal headdress/crown. Although there is some debate about what the entire request specifically entailed, the story records that she refuses to obey the order. After all, she was hosting her own banquet! Nevertheless, a king's command must be obeyed or dire consequences ensue for breaking the law.

After consultation with advisers, King Xerxes removes Vashti from her position as his queen and banishes her from his presence. Vashti's refusal to wear the crown will result in loss of power and rank, and an edict will be sent to all of the king's provinces that women should respect their husbands. The king's adviser, Memukan, might actually be in fear for his own household, as he worries for an uprising of "Persian women of nobility." Out of fear, an edict is sent to all of King Xerxes' provinces.

HADASSAH

Esther 2:1-2, 5-10, 17

Although this part of the story has been misunderstood as a beauty contest for the next Queen of Persia, it is actually a scene where young women are taken against their wills. The edict that went out in chapter 1 will be mirrored in scope to request all the beautiful young virgins in all the provinces of Persia to be taken to the citadel of Susa.

The story now centers on the experience of a young Jewish woman, Hadassah (Heb. myrtle), who is also known as Esther (Persian: star). Esther is an orphan being raised by her cousin, Mordecai, in the citadel of Susa. Mordecai is from the tribe of Benjamin, whose family was exiled by the Babylonian king, Nebuchadnezzar. Esther is "beautiful" and has a "lovely figure." This description is also used of Jacob's wife, Rachel (Genesis 29:17) and Abigail, Nabal's wife (1 Samuel

25:3), who later becomes the wife of David. Esther is taken to be placed under the care of Hegai, to be given beauty treatments along with the other women. The women taken would all become concubines for the king, while one would be chosen for the position of the next queen. Aware of potential danger in revealing Esther's ethnic and religious identity, Esther obeys her cousin Mordecai and keeps her background a secret (2:10). The text reveals that Esther receives favor *(hesed)* from Hegai (2:9), and later favor from everyone (2:15), and finally, she gained favor and approval from the king (2:17). Esther will move from the house of the women to the king's house. King Xerxes will choose as his next queen, Esther, by placing the royal headdress upon her.

Though God appears hidden through this story, Esther has gained the favor of everyone she comes into contact with. Esther is experiencing something she has not chosen. In an ancient society where a woman's rights are limited or nonexistent, it is essential to recall the oppressiveness and loss of identity Esther experienced in her situation. Nevertheless, God is with Esther, even in the darkest moments of her life.

Think About It

Vashti appears very briefly in the story of Esther. As the queen, she defies the king's order on the final day of the banquet. Rabbinic writers speculate that Vashti's refusal was due to the fact that she was requested to appear before the king with only her headdress/crown on and no clothes. Vashti's honor is never discussed, but her refusal makes a strong point. In a society with women's limited rights, Vashti takes a strong stand for herself and for women, losing her title, and her power as queen, and she could have risked her life as well. What is worth a risk in your life of faith?

REFLECT Pray, asking God to open your eyes to His moving presence in your life.

JENNIFER MATHENY is former professor at Nazarene Theological Seminary and currently serves as associate professor of Christian Scriptures at George W. Truett Seminary—Baylor University.

ACCEPTING YOUR GOD-GIVEN ROLE

God gives each of us opportunity to decide if we will become part of His redemptive plan.

THE WORD

ESTHER 3:8-10

Then Haman said to King Xerxes, "There is a certain people dispersed among the peoples in all the provinces of your kingdom who keep themselves separate. Their customs are different from those of all other people, and they do not obey the king's laws; it is not in the king's best interest to tolerate them. 9If it pleases the king, let a decree be issued to destroy them, and I will give ten thousand talents of silver to the king's administrators for the royal treasury."

10So the king took his signet ring from his finger and gave it to Haman son of Hammedatha, the Agagite, the enemy of the Jews.

ESTHER 4:5-16

5Then Esther summoned Hathak, one of the king's eunuchs assigned to attend her, and ordered him to find out what was troubling Mordecai and why.

6So Hathak went out to Mordecai in the open square of the city in front of the king's gate. 7Mordecai told him everything that had happened to him, including the exact amount of money Haman had promised to pay into the royal treasury for the destruction of the Jews. 8He also gave him a copy of the text of the edict for their annihilation, which had been published in Susa, to show to Esther and explain it to her, and he told him to instruct her to go into the king's presence to beg for mercy and plead with him for her people.

9Hathak went back and reported to Esther what Mordecai had said. 10Then she instructed him to say to Mordecai, 11"All the king's officials and the people of the royal provinces know that for any man or woman who approaches the king in the inner court without being summoned the king has but one law: that they be put to death unless

the king extends the gold scepter to them and spares their lives. But
thirty days have passed since I was called to go to the king."
[12]When Esther's words were reported to Mordecai, [13]he sent back
this answer: "Do not think that because you are in the king's house
you alone of all the Jews will escape. [14]For if you remain silent at this
time, relief and deliverance for the Jews will arise from another place,
but you and your father's family will perish. And who knows but that
you have come to your royal position for such a time as this?"

KEY VERSES

**[15]Then Esther sent this reply to Mordecai: [16]"Go, gather
together all the Jews who are in Susa, and fast for me. Do not eat
or drink for three days, night or day. I and my attendants will fast
as you do. When this is done, I will go to the king, even though it
is against the law. And if I perish, I perish."**

ENGAGE THE WORD

In this portion of the Esther story, an important character enters the scene: Haman the Agagite. King Xerxes honors Haman and gives him "a seat of honor higher than all the others" (Esther 3:1). The insertion of Haman's background with its connection to the Amalekites (Agagites, descended from Agag, king of the Amalekites) reveals an important plot twist. That is, Esther is a queen whose Jewish identity is currently hidden and the king's right-hand man is an Amalekite, a group of people who hold animosity for the Jewish people (Exodus 17). In a moment during the king's public honor for Haman, Mordecai refuses to bow down to Haman. After questioning, the officials give a reason for Mordecai's refusal to bow down, because "he is a Jew" (Esther 3:4). Haman's position of power and influence enables him to take intentional and devious measures to address Mordecai's obstinance and use it as a tool for oppression for the entire Jewish population.

HAMAN'S PLOT

Esther 3:8-10

Haman works a plot to twist partial truths to stir King Xerxes into action against an entire Jewish people. In Esther 1, Memukan's public discourse against

Did You Know?

The book of Esther shares themes and similarities with many other books in the Christian canon. Esther and Ruth are the only two books named after women. Esther and Daniel share a similar storyline—both books detail life in exile and how the Jews flourish under foreign rule. Many themes parallel Joseph's life in Genesis, most notably in their difficult origin stories of loss and subsequent rise to power in a foreign land!

Vashti's actions result in a royal decree, meant to serve as warning for all wives (Esther 1:20). Similarly, Haman will levy one action of disrespect for possible annihilation of an entire people. Haman presents no solid confirmation that would warrant the king's decree, but Haman has learned how to manipulate the king and the king plays right into his hands. Haman advances the rhetoric that the Jews are different, disobedient, and keep themselves separate. Haman twists this to be a threat to the empire. Persian law allowed for diverse ethnic and religious groups to maintain adherence to their own laws. However, Haman finds a way to use this to incite the king's power and influence. He quickly offers a plan to remedy the problem to the narrative he has spun.

The king transfers a new power level to Haman as he removes the signet ring from his hand and bestows it into Haman's hand. Haman used this ring of power to send out a decree to all the king's provinces and in all the diverse languages of the Persian empire. Haman's intention is revealed in the edict and is absurdly disproportionate to Mordecai's actions. Haman commands a complete holocaust of the Jewish people. The decree commands people everywhere on the 13th day of the 12th month to destroy, to kill, and to annihilate every Jewish person, from young to the elderly.

MORDECAI MOURNS, ESTHER ACTS

Esther 4:5-16

Mordecai hears about the edict to destroy the Jewish people and changes his clothes into articles and elements of mourning: sackcloth and ashes (Esther 4:1-3). Esther hears about Mordecai mourning and, through her attendants, sends him a different set of clothes, but he refuses to put them on (Esther 3:4). This moment leads to Esther finding out about Haman's decree. Esther may be queen, but she is not privy to all the happenings around the province.

The knowledge of Esther's people on the verge of

Think About It

Esther's origin story details her life as one of orphan raised by her cousin, Mordecai. The text does not go into detail about Esther's internal life, but it can be helpful to think about how she may have responded to possible danger as an adult after being a child who was orphaned. Esther may have desired to remain safe and hidden in the palace's protection after so much family loss. Do you think her origin story encouraged her bravery or made her boldness more difficult?

destruction becomes a moment of risk and possibility. Mordecai wisely asks, "And who knows but that you have come to your royal position for such a time as this?" (Esther 4:14b). Esther sends the message to Mordecai to call all Jews to fast and pray before she acts. Her identity as a Jewish woman has been hidden, but it is about to be revealed at possible peril. To approach the king unannounced can mean certain death. Esther's life hangs in the balance through one item of dress, the king's golden scepter. If it is extended to her, Esther will be able to approach the king. If not, she will be executed.

The transfer of an item of clothing is an important motif in the Esther story as it constructs and deconstructs power. In Esther 1, we see this movement with Queen Vashti's refusal to wear the headdress and her status moves from Queen Vashti (Esther 1:12) to Vashti (Esther 1:19). This headdress is placed upon Esther's head to "make her queen instead of Vashti" (Esther 2:17b). Here in Esther 3, the signet ring transfers from the hand of King Xerxes to Haman. The result of the power transfer is a decree that leaves the city of Susa confused and bewildered (Esther 3:15). Esther responds to the edict through a call for prayer and fasting. Although God is not mentioned in this story, God's hidden presence is revealed through the actions of God's people.

REFLECT Is there a current situation that might lead you to prayer and fasting?

JENNIFER MATHENY

GOD HONORS HIS SERVANT

God surprises His people with honor and His enemies with justice.

THE WORD

ESTHER 5:11-14

Haman boasted to them about his vast wealth, his many sons, and
all the ways the king had honored him and how he had elevated
him above the other nobles and officials. [12]"And that's not all," Haman
added. "I'm the only person Queen Esther invited to accompany the
king to the banquet she gave. And she has invited me along with the
king tomorrow. [13]But all this gives me no satisfaction as long as I see
that Jew Mordecai sitting at the king's gate."

[14]His wife Zeresh and all his friends said to him, "Have a pole
set up, reaching to a height of fifty cubits, and ask the king in the
morning to have Mordecai impaled on it. Then go with the king to the
banquet and enjoy yourself." This suggestion delighted Haman, and
he had the pole set up.

ESTHER 6:1-10

[1]That night the king could not sleep; so he ordered the book of
the chronicles, the record of his reign, to be brought in and read to
him. [2]It was found recorded there that Mordecai had exposed Bigtha-
na and Teresh, two of the king's officers who guarded the doorway,
who had conspired to assassinate King Xerxes.

[3]"What honor and recognition has Mordecai received for this?"
the king asked.

"Nothing has been done for him," his attendants answered.

[4]The king said, "Who is in the court?" Now Haman had just entered the outer court of the palace to speak to the king about impaling
Mordecai on the pole he had set up for him.

[5]His attendants answered, "Haman is standing in the court."

"Bring him in," the king ordered.

[6]When Haman entered, the king asked him, "What should be done for the man the king delights to honor?"

Now Haman thought to himself, "Who is there that the king would rather honor than me?" [7]So he answered the king, "For the man the king delights to honor, [8]have them bring a royal robe the king has worn and a horse the king has ridden, one with a royal crest placed on its head. [9]Then let the robe and horse be entrusted to one of the king's most noble princes. Let them robe the man the king delights to honor, and lead him on the horse through the city streets, proclaiming before him, 'This is what is done for the man the king delights to honor!'"

KEY VERSE

[10]"Go at once," the king commanded Haman. "Get the robe and the horse and do just as you have suggested for Mordecai the Jew, who sits at the king's gate. Do not neglect anything you have recommended."

ENGAGE THE WORD

Esther 5 marks a key scene and turning point for Esther. Esther puts on her royalty and stands in the inner court of the palace, ready to enter the king's hall. Here, the text calls her Esther (Esther 5:1), but once she changes into her royal robes, she becomes "Queen Esther" (Esther 5:2). In this moment she stands on behalf of all of her people.

The king favors Esther and he extends his golden scepter. This movement indicates life and hope, not only for Esther, but all of the Jewish people. The king has so much favor for Esther that he asks her request and he offers up to half of his kingdom! Wisdom is revealed through Esther as she carefully navigates this generous offer.

HAMAN'S ARROGANCE

Esther 5:11-14

Haman's pride comes on full display as he brags about his invitation to the banquet Esther has prepared for him and the king. He brags about his wealth, his position, and his power to his family. He also had a run in with Mordecai earlier and, fueled with rage, erects poles to have Mordecai impaled upon. Haman

Did You Know?

Cloth and clothing in Esther are presented to the limits of excess. Reading with an eye towards extravagance adds to this court narrative's literary beauty and complexity. Language of opulence through clothing is seen through 12 key scenes with important characters including Xerxes, Vashti, Esther, Mordecai, and Haman (1:6; 1:11; 2:17; 3:12; 4:1-4; 4:11; 5:1; 5:2; 6:6-11; 8:2; 8:4; 8:15).

is infuriated that Mordecai did not rise in this scene (Esther 5:9). Literary irony is at play in Esther 5, as Mordecai neither bows (3:2) nor rises (5:9) before Haman to show respect. Haman's mind is obsessed with Mordecai's irreverence for him. The violence in his heart for Mordecai and the Jewish people become publicly visible as he erects this immense pole, 50 cubits high (around 75 feet)! Haman is intensely focused on the one thing he cannot have or control. Obsessive ruminations can make one miss out on the many good things all around.

UNEXPECTED HONOREE

Esther 6:1-10

Even though God is not overtly named in the story, it becomes clear that God orchestrates justice and honor in surprising an unforeseen ways. In Esther 6, honor comes into the fore and full circle in this chapter. In chapter 1, the king's honor is a key theme in the decree given after Vashti's act of refusal to come before the king in her headdress/crown. We also see this in Memukan's concern for the king's honor (Esther 1:20) and even his greatness. Honor continues to resurface here in the narrative, as well as, irony and reversals.

The king cannot sleep and requests for the book of annals to be read to him, perhaps in hopes this will calm his mind to sleep. Here we also see the providence of God come into play . . . for a king and his attendants focused on honor, one of the stories read is about Mordecai! Mordecai averted an assassination plot against the king and was never honored! Haman is summoned to help the king out with this quandary. Haman's pride is glaring in this moment. The king asks Haman what he should do for "a man the king desires to honor" (Esther 6:6). Haman immediately hears honor and assumes the king is talking about him! Haman is all about Haman. This phrase, "the man the king desires to honor" is referred to three times in this chapter (Esther 6:6, 7, 9). Oh the irony of who deserves honor!

Think About It

The story of Esther, the story of Joseph (Genesis 37—50), and Daniel 1—6, share important characteristics. These stories have been called court narratives, a common genre of writing in the ancient Near East context. Reading them together can be fascinating as they each detail life under a foreign ruler and seek to illustrate diverse ways to live out the complexities of a life of faith and loyalty to God under difficult circumstances.

Haman presents an extravagant plan to honor this "one the king desires to honor." Haman imagines that there is no one else in the entire Persian provinces that deserves honor more than himself (Esther 6:6b)!

The clothing motif plays into the irony of reversals in the following scenes. Haman suggests a change of clothes for this honored one, the kings royal robes. The "royal crest" on the horse is the royal headdress or crown. This headdress reminds the reader of the one worn by Vashti and Esther (Esther 1:11; 2:17) and the royal robes Esther places on herself before she courageously stood before the king in the inner court (Esther 5:1). To Haman's dismay, his elaborate suggestions will result in honor displayed with royal robes upon Mordecai, a royal headdress on the horse, and Haman himself parading his enemy, Mordecai, around Susa! (Clearly, and ironically, Haman's request for a horse the king has ridden reveals his ambitions.)

This kingly moment turns dramatically as Haman hears the honoree named: Mordecai. The reversals Haman begins to experience he shares with his family. His celebratory mood changes to a "head covered in grief" (Esther 6:12) as he joins the king at the second banquet Esther has prepared.

REFLECT Do not take revenge, my dear friends, but leave room for God's wrath, for it is written: 'It is mine to avenge; I will repay,' says the Lord" (Romans 12:19).

JENNIFER MATHENY

A DISCERNING QUEEN

God gives wisdom to His faithful as they fight against the evil of this world.

THE WORD

ESTHER 5:1-5

On the third day Esther put on her royal robes and stood in the inner court of the palace, in front of the king's hall. The king was sitting on his royal throne in the hall, facing the entrance. [2] When he saw Queen Esther standing in the court, he was pleased with her and held out to her the gold scepter that was in his hand. So Esther approached and touched the tip of the scepter.

[3]Then the king asked, "What is it, Queen Esther? What is your request? Even up to half the kingdom, it will be given you."

[4]"If it pleases the king," replied Esther, "let the king, together with Haman, come today to a banquet I have prepared for him."

[5]"Bring Haman at once," the king said, "so that we may do what Esther asks."

So the king and Haman went to the banquet Esther had prepared.

ESTHER 7:1-6

[1]So the king and Haman went to Queen Esther's banquet, [2]and as they were drinking wine on the second day, the king again asked, "Queen Esther, what is your petition? It will be given you. What is your request? Even up to half the kingdom, it will be granted."

KEY VERSE

[3]Then Queen Esther answered, "If I have found favor with you, Your Majesty, and if it pleases you, grant me my life—this is my petition. And spare my people—this is my request. [4]For I and my people have been sold to be destroyed, killed and annihilated. If we had merely been sold as male and female slaves, I would have kept quiet, because no such distress would justify disturbing the king."

[5]King Xerxes asked Queen Esther, "Who is he? Where is he—the man who has dared to do such a thing?"

[6]Esther said, "An adversary and enemy! This vile Haman!"
Then Haman was terrified before the king and queen.

9-10 [9]Then Harbona, one of the eunuchs attending the king, said, "A
pole reaching to a height of fifty cubits stands by Haman's house. He
had it set up for Mordecai, who spoke up to help the king."
The king said, "Impale him on it!" [10]So they impaled Haman on
the pole he had set up for Mordecai. Then the king's fury subsided.

ENGAGE THE WORD

A WOMAN OF PRAYER AND COURAGE

Esther 5:1-5

Esther didn't abandon her people—she stood up for them, identified herself with them, and took action on their behalf. As a woman in Persian society, Esther had very little power and few individual rights. By virtue of her position as queen, she had some influence.

Esther is a woman of prayer and courage. In Esther 5, Esther immediately calls for prayer and fasting when she hears about the decree to annihilate her people. After three days, she dresses in her royal robes and approaches the king. Receiving his favor, Esther wisely sets up a series of banquets before she makes her formal request. Between these two banquets, a turn of events has occurred with the honoring of Mordecai.

In a seemingly hopeless situation, God has been at work. This is a reminder to hope and pray against the visible/material (and spiritual) forces that are opposed to God's people. Even when there appears to be no way through a difficult or even oppressive situation, God creatively acts through unconventional means, like a king's insomnia (6:1).

ESTHER'S REQUEST

Esther 7:1-6, 9-10

Esther's second banquet mirrors the first. The question from the king remains the same, "Queen Esther, what is your petition? It will be given you. What is your request? Even up to half the kingdom, it will be granted" (Esther 7:2). Similar to Esther 5:3, the king refers

Did You Know?

One of the disturbing moments in the Esther story is when Haman devises a scheme to destroy the Jewish people and King Xerxes gives Haman the power to go forth with his plan without ever seeking out details about who these particular people are in his kingdom (Esther 3:1-11). King Xerxes is portrayed as a leader who can be swayed, is self-indulgent, and fueled by his carnal desires. Fortunately, the tales of reversal will turn in favor of God's people and God will use Esther to turn the motivation of this king in their favor.

to Esther as "Queen Esther." In this moment, Esther is ready to boldly make the request. Esther addresses the king respectfully and with honor. In this request, Esther will add to it a request for her life and for the life of her people to be spared. Using the language of servitude, Esther says that she and her people have been sold to be completely wiped out (7:4).

Haman's initial approach to the king in Esther 3 was an attractive offer...weaving a tale of profit and honor to gain the king's favor in issuing the edict against the Jewish people. Esther repurposes similar language that Haman used in Esther 3. Esther says, "For I and my people have been sold to be destroyed, killed and annihilated. If we had merely been sold as male and female slaves, I would have kept quiet, because no such distress would justify disturbing the king" (Esther 7:4). The language used here of being "sold" brings up intertextual allusion to the story of Joseph being sold by his brothers in Genesis 37:28, 36, and 45:4.

King Xerxes takes in all Esther has spoken and is rightly enraged. He immediately asks who has threatened his queen and her people. Esther responds, "An adversary and enemy! This vile Haman!" The writer has already indicated in Esther 3 that Haman is the "foe/enemy" of the Jews. Here, at this moment in time, Haman is not only the enemy of the Jews, but he is also Esther's enemy and the king's! The king recuses himself to the garden in his anger. Haman stays behind with Esther to plead for his life.

Haman "stands" in this scene to plead for Esther to save his life. Before the king returns, Haman is lying prostrate before Esther. Upon the king's return, he sees Haman lying near Esther and the king accuses Haman of sexually advancing upon the queen while the king is "in the house." Some scholars wonder if perhaps the king accuses Haman of this inappropriate posture to have a reason to punish him immediately. This moment is the apex of irony, a scene filled with Haman being dishonored. The Hebrew text states that

Think About It

Esther displays strong connections to wisdom literature. In wisdom literature, groups of people can be seen as "types" or "typecast," such as "the wicked" and "the righteous." If you begin to read Proverbs, these "types" become evident very quickly. The story of Job provides a helpful counterbalance to an overly simplified typecast of individuals. Reading books like these together is important to encompass a broader and more complex outlook on life and theology.

Haman is accused of conquering the queen. What a plot twist! Haman has tried to conquer, to destroy the Jews. In a swift turn of events, Haman will be impaled on the pole he built for Mordecai.

This final scene brings a close to the animosity between Mordecai and Haman. The narrative brilliantly uses confusion and misinterpretation of events to raise the level of irony and humor. In chapter 6, Haman misunderstands who the king desires to honor. Here in chapter 7, the king misinterprets (intentionally?) Haman's posture before Esther. Adele Berlin writes, "The irony is that now both Esther and Ahasuerus have accused Haman of gross insubordination–of wishing to supplant the king . . .Haman's lust for honor has at last been laid bare, and it proves his undoing."[1]

1. Adele Berlin. *Esther: THE JPS Bible Commentary* (Philadelphia: Jewish Publication Society, 2001), 64-65.

REFLECT In what ways can you intercede on behalf of those who are facing injustice?

JENNIFER MATHENY

GOD DELIVERS HIS PEOPLE

God makes a way for His people to overcome the enemies of His kingdom.

THE WORD

ESTHER 8:3-13

Esther again pleaded with the king, falling at his feet and weeping. She begged him to put an end to the evil plan of Haman the Agagite, which he had devised against the Jews. [4]Then the king extended the gold scepter to Esther and she arose and stood before him.

[5]"If it pleases the king," she said, "and if he regards me with favor and thinks it the right thing to do, and if he is pleased with me, let an order be written overruling the dispatches that Haman son of Hammedatha, the Agagite, devised and wrote to destroy the Jews in all the king's provinces. [6]For how can I bear to see disaster fall on my people? How can I bear to see the destruction of my family?"

[7]King Xerxes replied to Queen Esther and to Mordecai the Jew, "Because Haman attacked the Jews, I have given his estate to Esther, and they have impaled him on the pole he set up. [8]Now write another decree in the king's name in behalf of the Jews as seems best to you, and seal it with the king's signet ring—for no document written in the king's name and sealed with his ring can be revoked."

[9]At once the royal secretaries were summoned—on the twenty-third day of the third month, the month of Sivan. They wrote out all Mordecai's orders to the Jews, and to the satraps, governors and nobles of the 127 provinces stretching from India to Cush. These orders were written in the script of each province and the language of each people and also to the Jews in their own script and language. [10]Mordecai wrote in the name of King Xerxes, sealed the dispatches with the king's signet ring, and sent them by mounted couriers, who rode fast horses especially bred for the king.

[11]The king's edict granted the Jews in every city the right to

assemble and protect themselves; to destroy, kill and annihilate the armed men of any nationality or province who might attack them and their women and children, and to plunder the property of their enemies. [12]The day appointed for the Jews to do this in all the provinces of King Xerxes was the thirteenth day of the twelfth month, the month

KEY VERSE

of Adar. **[13]A copy of the text of the edict was to be issued as law in every province and made known to the people of every nationality so that the Jews would be ready on that day to avenge themselves on their enemies.**

ENGAGE THE WORD

REVERSALS

Esther 8:3-13

Esther's courage and agency to plead for her people continues in this chapter. Her personal world was safe. She could have accepted the gift of Haman's property for her family and allowed herself to be insulated in the safety of the palace in Susa. Instead, Esther risks her life for her people. Because the king gave the edict, it could not be revoked. Esther now brings her cousin Mordecai before the king. Together, this unsuspecting Jewish family will now have power and influence, even in exile. The ways of God are profound! King Xerxes gives Mordecai his signet ring. What a reversal! Originally on Haman's hand, now Mordecai has charge over Haman's estate and the signet ring. The theme of reversals is woven all throughout Esther 8.

Scholars demonstrate the literary artistry of the book of Esther. In chapter 8, language is reused for emphasis and many phrases are parallel to chapter 3.

Here are a few examples of reversals and repetition:

- The repeated phrase: "Haman, the 'enemy' of the Jews" (3:10; 8:1)
- Mordecai is given Haman's property and Mordecai is brought before the king, like Haman (3:1; 8:1-2).
- The king's signet ring is given to Haman (3:10). The king's signet ring is given to Mordecai (8:2)
- An edict is given to destroy the Jews (3:13-15). An edict is given to allow the Jews to defend themselves (8:11)

Did You Know?

Esther is part of a group of scrolls in Jewish tradition called the *Megillot* (five scrolls). This group of scrolls include Ruth, Lamentations, Song of Songs, and Ecclesiastes (Qohelet). In the Tiberian ordering of books, these five scrolls begin with Ruth and ends with Esther (Ruth, Songs, Qohelet, Lamentations, Esther). Each scroll connects to one of the five major holidays of the Jewish liturgical year.

- The people of Susa are bewildered at the edict (3:15). The Jews of Susa rejoice at the new edict (8:17).

The language of both edicts is violent. In the first edict in Esther 3, the instructions are to destroy, to kill, and to annihilate every Jewish person, including women and children! Here in Esther 8, literary reversals are seen in the new edict. The Jewish people are given power to destroy, to kill, and to annihilate those who attack the Jews.

Because the old edict could not be reversed, the Jews could legally protect themselves in this dark hour. Some of the language is different than the first in the second edict. Mordecai's instructions call for the Jewish people to "assemble" and to "protect" themselves. In the Hebrew this is "to stand for their lives." What is also notable is that unlike the first edict that calls for the people of Persia to attack the Jews; here, the Jewish people are to attack the "armed forces" that are coming against them. The language indicates agency for the Jews to defend themselves. The harsh language of the second edict parallels the first and is meant to match the intensity of attack with intensity to defend. The edict is quickly sent on the 23rd day of Sivan, the third month. There are less than 9 months to get the word out.

When Esther is read, the focus is often on Esther's rise to power and the personal risk she took to save the Jewish people. Reading through this story more slowly, it becomes evident that there is much violence in this story. This can be one of the difficult realities when reading the Old Testament. It is helpful to remember that these are very ancient stories within an ancient Near Eastern context. One helpful reading strategy is to step back and think about where God has worked through the lives of people and individuals in very difficult situations.

In Esther 9:17b it states that, "And many people of other nationalities became Jews because fear of the

Think About It

Thinking about Esther as part of a group of scrolls celebrated through the Jewish liturgical year, it becomes apparent that theology is embodied through practices which include reading, singing, celebration, and even fasting. Michael LeFebvre writes that festivals do not serve the "chronology of history but the cadence of worship."[1] What are important rhythms for you in the Christian calendar year that inspire you to live out your theology in community? What are key practices (e.g., celebrations, fasting, worship) that you find meaningful?

Jews had seized them." This verse has been a source of scholarly discussion as you might imagine. Was there conversion out of fear? This does not resonate well with our modern care and commitment to evangelism! In the Hebrew, the non-Jewish people are referred to as "people of the land." One translation states that this could be "they identified themselves with the Jews" (Levenson) or "sided with the Jews" (Berlin). So rather than conversion, this verse could mean that the people of the land took the side of the Jews and defended them against their attackers. This is not to say that there were not converts to Judaism. We see this all throughout the Old Testament.

God's heart desires peace and care for our neighbors. The reality is that this is not always lived out. Haman sought to destroy God's people and issued an edict that could not be reversed. Recalling Esther's rise to power, she risked violence upon herself to save her people. Risking the life of one to save a group is the heart of sacrifice and love for neighbor. Haman authored a death notice for the Jews. Esther and Mordecai found a way to protect the lives of the Jewish people. God makes a way for His people to overcome the enemies of God's kingdom!

1. Michael LeFebvre. *The Liturgy of Creation* (Westmont: IVP Academic, 2019), 93.

REFLECT In what ways have you seen God's protection in the lives of His faithful followers?

JENNIFER MATHENY

CELEBRATING GOD'S MERCY

God's people should remember and celebrate important moments of God's amazing mercy and grace.

THE WORD

ESTHER 9:20-32

Mordecai recorded these events, and he sent letters to all the
Jews throughout the provinces of King Xerxes, near and far, [21]to
have them celebrate annually the fourteenth and fifteenth days of
the month of Adar [22]as the time when the Jews got relief from their
enemies, and as the month when their sorrow was turned into joy and
their mourning into a day of celebration. He wrote them to observe
the days as days of feasting and joy and giving presents of food to
one another and gifts to the poor.

[23]So the Jews agreed to continue the celebration they had begun,
doing what Mordecai had written to them. [24]For Haman son of Hammedatha, the Agagite, the enemy of all the Jews, had plotted against
the Jews to destroy them and had cast the pur (that is, the lot) for
their ruin and destruction. [25]But when the plot came to the king's
attention, he issued written orders that the evil scheme Haman had
devised against the Jews should come back onto his own head, and
that he and his sons should be impaled on poles. [26](Therefore these
days were called Purim, from the word pur.) Because of everything
written in this letter and because of what they had seen and what had
happened to them, [27]the Jews took it on themselves to establish the
custom that they and their descendants and all who join them should
without fail observe these two days every year, in the way prescribed
and at the time appointed. **[28]These days should be remembered
and observed in every generation by every family, and in every
province and in every city. And these days of Purim should never
fail to be celebrated by the Jews—nor should the memory of
these days die out among their descendants.**

KEY VERSE

[29]So Queen Esther, daughter of Abihail, along with Mordecai the
Jew, wrote with full authority to confirm this second letter concerning
Purim. [30]And Mordecai sent letters to all the Jews in the 127 provinces of Xerxes' kingdom—words of goodwill and assurance— [31]to
establish these days of Purim at their designated times, as Mordecai
the Jew and Queen Esther had decreed for them, and as they had
established for themselves and their descendants in regard to their
times of fasting and lamentation. [32]Esther's decree confirmed these
regulations about Purim, and it was written down in the records.

ENGAGE THE WORD

In Exodus, the Israelites are commanded to observe the Passover every year to remember that God delivered them out of Egypt. It is to be a time to remember all God has done for His people; it is a time to celebrate God's mighty acts and look forward to how He will act in the future. Throughout the Bible, the call to God's people is always to remember. To remember who they belong to, to remember what their God has done.

A TIME OF REMEMBERING

Esther 9:20-32

Advent is a season of expectant waiting in the rhythms of the Christian liturgical year, a time where the people of God wait in anticipation for the celebration of Jesus' coming, "God with us" (Matthew 1:23). Seasons of the church help communities reflect on the most important seasonal rhythms of life, reflecting on how these ancient stories of God continue to give life and sustain the church in creative and vibrant ways through these celebratory rhythms. The church needs to remember the ways and wonders of God as it engages with present realities and struggles.

Here in Esther, a difficult space of waiting ensues. Haman has been dealt with, but the edict to destroy the Jews could not be revoked. Esther and Mordecai proceed to intervene in this perilous space and create a counter edict that enables the Jews to defend themselves against armed attackers. As we witnessed in

Did You Know?

One of the earliest accounts of Purim is from 2 Maccabees (late second century BC). Unlike other pilgrimage festivals commanded in the Torah (e.g., Passover and the Festival of Unleavened Bread, Festival of Weeks, Festival of Tabernacles), no sacrifice or offerings are commanded. Its origin is attributed to the book of Esther.

the previous session, the Lord makes a way for God's people to overcome the enemies of God's kingdom.

Here in Esther 9, the Jews take a stand against those seeking their harm. The Jews were not alone in their defense! "No one could stand against them, because the people of all the other nationalities feared them. And all the nobles of the provinces, the satraps, the governors and the king's administrators helped the Jews, because fear of Mordecai had seized them" (Esther 9:2b-3). The great reversal of Haman's original plot to impale Mordecai now takes an even greater turn of events as Mordecai is "growing powerful" (Esther 9:4b). As the fighting ensues, notice that Haman's edict in Esther 3 allowed for the enemies to take spoils from the Jews. Mordecai's counter edict allows for this as well. This is routine in ancient warfare. As you read through Esther 9, notice that the Jews were permitted by the edict to take spoils after triumphing over their attackers; even so, the text says that the Jews "did not lay hands on the spoil" (Esther 9:10b). They protected themselves, but did not seek economic gain from the situation.

Esther will seek to make another request before the king. This adds a comedic element to the story as the reader is aware that Esther shall be given whatever she asks for! She has the king's favor and this will enable her to seek favor on behalf of the Jewish people once more. Her request is in two parts, (1) an extension of one day for the Jews in Susa to defend themselves and (2) for Haman's 10 sons to be impaled on poles. This public display serves as a warning to any sectors of resistance who seek to harm the Jewish people.

The bold request of Queen Esther results in the Jewish community of Persia being saved! In order to remember the events, the festival of Purim is established and celebrated every year (Esther 9:20-28).

"These days should be remembered and observed in every generation by every family, and in every province

Think About It

As you enter the Advent season this year, how are you preparing your heart as a place of waiting *and* welcoming? Romans 15:7 encourages us to "Welcome one another, therefore, just as Christ has welcomed you, for the glory of God" (NRSV).

and in every city. And these days of Purim should never fail to be celebrated by the Jews—nor should the memory of these days die out among their descendants" (Esther 9:28).

Purim derives from the Persian word, *pur*, meaning "lots" or "lottery." (Haman cast lots to decide which day his violent edict would be carried out. See Esther 9:24.) Purim is a festival to celebrate how the Jews obtained "rest" from their enemies and victory over their foes. Purim is celebrated by feasts (eating and drinking), giving gifts, and displays of rejoicing! Today, Purim is still celebrated in a carnivalesque manner with costumes, merry making, special foods, and gifts.

Throughout the Old Testament, God invites Israel to "remember." The Ten Words (commandments) in Exodus 20 begin with God reminding Israel that God brought them out of Egypt. A few verses down, God invites Israel to "remember the Sabbath" (Exodus 20:8).

Remembering our story as God's people through the liturgical year is not just something good to do, but it is essential in recalling our story and remembering our identity as God's people. More than reminiscing, celebrating the works of God continues to root us in our true identity as God's holy people, a people God has created, loves, and sends into this world to share the good news! It is too easy to forget who we are and whose we are; therefore, let us always remember!

REFLECT

In what ways do you remember and celebrate important moments of God's amazing mercy and grace?

JENNIFER MATHENY

Printed in the USA
CPSIA information can be obtained
at www.ICGtesting.com
LVHW081029100924
790656LV00020B/454